NOW I KNOW™
Turtles

by MELVIN AND GILDA BERGER

SCHOLASTIC INC.

New York   Toronto   London   Auckland   Sydney
Mexico City   New Delhi   Hong Kong   Buenos Aires

Which animal carries its home on its back?

The turtle does.

It has a hard shell.

There are many kinds of turtles.

Some turtles live on land.

They walk on four legs.

ZOOM!

The box turtle lives on land.

ZOOM!

It can pull its head
and legs into its shell.

Some turtles are pond turtles.

They hide in the mud.

The snapping turtle
is a pond turtle.

It has a very big head.

Some turtles live in the sea.

Sea turtles have four flippers
instead of legs.

The green turtle is a sea turtle.

It swims very fast.

Land turtles have high shells.

Sea turtles have flat shells.

Some turtles eat plants.

Some eat little animals.

All turtles hatch from eggs.

ZOOM!

DID YOU KNOW?
Female sea turtles only come to land to lay their eggs.

The mother buries the eggs on land.

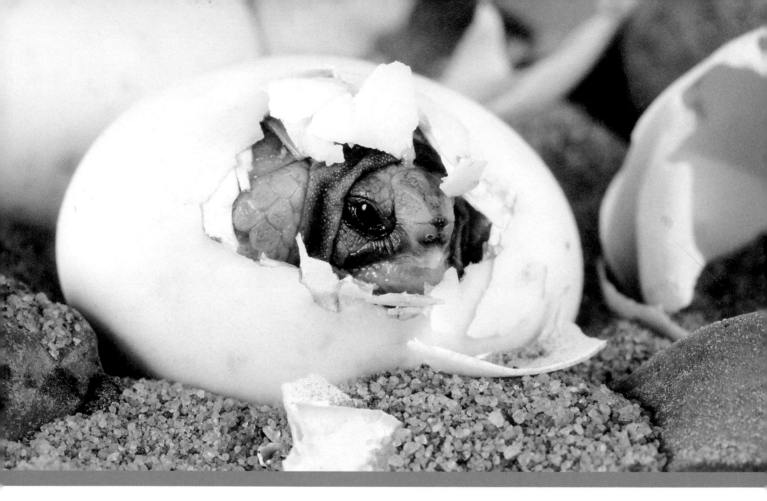

The sun warms the eggs.
The turtles start to hatch.

ZOOM!

Here come the babies!

Some hide in the water.

Some hide on land.

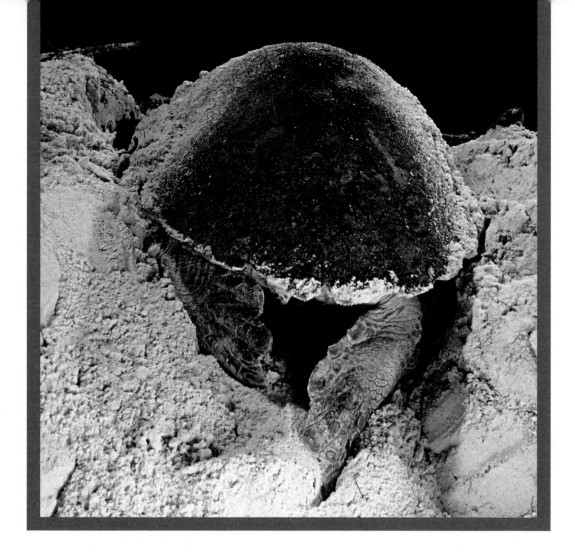

But they all carry homes on their backs!

GLOSSARY

Box turtle: A land turtle. A box turtle can tightly close the top and bottom parts of its shell.

Egg: The first step in the life of a turtle. Baby turtles hatch from eggs.

Flippers: The flat legs of a sea turtle. A sea turtle moves its flippers up and down to swim.

Green turtle: A sea turtle. Green turtles swim in warm ocean waters.

Hatch: To break out of an egg. Turtles hatch about 2 or 3 months after the female lays the eggs.

Land turtle: A turtle that spends most of its time on the ground. The box turtle is a land turtle.

Pond turtle: A turtle that spends most of its time in ponds or other freshwater. The snapping turtle is a pond turtle.

Sea turtle: A turtle that lives in the sea or ocean. The green turtle is a sea turtle.

Shell: The hard outside covering of a turtle. A turtle's shell protects its body.

Snapping turtle: A pond turtle. The snapping turtle has strong jaws for catching food or fighting.

Turtles: A group of animals with shells that live on land or in water.